C000299349

Home Ed
&
Four Legs

A mess of happiness ♡

by Hannah Whyman-Naveh

First paperback edition January 2021

ISBN 978-1-8382058-1-2
(paperback)

HannahwhymannavehAuthor.com

Book cover designed by Fakenham Prepress Solutions
fakprepress.co.uk

Professional photography by Karla Davis
'Special Little Feet'
karladavisphotography.co.uk

Welcome to my honest and very personal experience of this amazing life called home ed,
Hannah x

4

Introduction

Introduction

Introduction

This book is not a home education 'how-to' guide. It is just a brutally honest account of my experiences in the past 20 months, both the good bits and the not-so-good bits, and what I have learnt along the way. I hope it doesn't offend anyone (actually it should do the opposite, although be warned I do drop the f-bomb occasionally!) and shows how home education is inclusive of all walks of life. This book is, in simple terms, for any human being who just feels school isn't right for their child, or is intrigued by home education.

At the time of writing this book, the country is on

the brink of being thrust into another Covid-19 lockdown (number 304 maybe? – I've lost count). It is January 2nd, 2021 in England, and a happy new year is looking just as reliable as my New Year's Eve resolution to lose weight. A vaccine is somewhere around the corner, but Christ knows when my age group will get it, or if it will actually work. Most of the country is in Tier 4, aka fuck-knows-if-we-stay-in-or-go-out. The world is a scary place with the daily rate of positive Covid tests going up, let alone the distant realisation that the death rate is at an all-time high.

It's also the time lots of you are about to send your kids back to school. Some parents can't wait, they have a life – don't know what kind of life that is at the moment, but hey, who wouldn't want six hours of free childcare a day? Some people are keyworkers and complete saints; for them, the childcare which school provides is essential, purely so they can keep the country running. I'm grateful to each and every one of them, very selfless people who send their children to school and go to work, knowing they really are on the front line. Without them this country would have taken a nose-dive into the Covid abyss.

There are some parents, however, who don't want to send their children back. They are worried about them getting Covid, or just making the situation worse. They are fighting an internal battle between sending the kids to school versus keeping them at home until normality resumes – but what if it doesn't? It's tough for parents at the moment and I can understand why some are looking at home education more closely.

If you are one of these people looking at home education for your family, then I hope this book offers some support and an insight into different styles of home ed, as well as my take on all the important things like deregistering and keeping in touch with your local authority.

I didn't find it hard to make the transition to home ed. I didn't need to jump through hoops and, contrary to the stereotype, us home edders aren't all quirky, dreadlock-loving, braless hippies with a pale-looking child attached to a breast (though hey, nothing wrong with that!). Some of us are just regular people who decided to take control of our children's education. That's it, basically. This is our normal, it is fun, free and fine-less – no more worrying about keeping children off school, as long as you are providing them with an education.

This book is not anti-government, it is not anti-school and is most certainly not anti-teacher (teachers deserve a fucking medal. FACT). I love teachers. Most strive to give the best possible education, but with at least 30-odd kids with different abilities, different learning techniques, different behaviours and different creativity in a class, no wonder they struggle. I am sure if you asked teachers, many would want a more home education style of learning in the classroom.

So, you're raising your kids without completely losing the plot, huh? Well, I'll see your non-plot losing, and I raise you HOME ED!

Why home education?

Why home
education?

Why home education?

This is always a tricky question to answer because the answer is different for everyone. Generally, everyone home educates for a reason: maybe their child has been bullied, or the parent feels let down by the school, or something along those lines. Maybe they home educate because they were home educated themselves, or maybe they just do it because they feel it is right for their child.

Life throws spanners in the works often and, trust me, home education was a huge spanner for our family. It was something I'd always felt intrigued by, but definitely not something I felt I was able to do, mainly because I thought I was too thick and partly because I thought only the stereotypical types of people did things like that. But I was utterly wrong, and when our eldest daughter, Poppy, became very withdrawn and came home from school sobbing and saying she was being bullied, I decided to take the plunge.

I live with my family – Idan, my husband, and our daughters Poppy, Indie Rose and Piper - on a small farm in Norfolk. It's a quirky little place, a small three-bedroom cottage. You know the type; tiny rooms with doors that don't fit the wonky doorways, and floors that could hold an elephant, while a wardrobe wobbles. It comes with a few acres of land next to it, plus we rent more acreage in the next village

Before the children arrived, Idan and I lived in a nearby village, in a simple house. We hated it. We couldn't wait to get more rural and out of the way, like we are now. Poppy was about three years old when we moved here and Indie was about 10 months. Even though we gave up owning to rent from an estate, I felt like a huge weight was lifted as soon as we picked up the keys, and that feeling has never left. It wasn't the prettiest of places when we moved in, there was a hell of a lot to do. Actually, I have come to the realisation that it's a work in progress and for that it will never be blooming finished.

My childhood was great and I was relatively happy at school. I was normal kid who went to normal schools and had normal parents (now known as

Nanny and Bubba). I had two, much older, brothers from my dad's side and a lot of family around me, and yet I was quite lonely as a child and I think that's probably why my memories of childhood are of the stables where I rode. I had so much fun when I was around horses and the yard girls became my sisters, but I hadn't realised this until I got much older.

I had some lovely school friends and I was never bullied, or no more than anyone else and definitely not to the level of bullying you see these days. I'm thankful there was no social media back then. I was a bit of a shit in my teens, I thought I was funny, but I wasn't. Still, it made for some fun conversations with teachers and pickles I had to wiggle myself out of. Again, all very normal, but I did fall out of school with barely a qualification.

When Poppy felt she was being bullied at school, it was a very worrying time for us as a family. Finding another school in the area was not an option, as she was already at the best school, and I felt her problems would probably just follow her wherever she went. She was in year five at primary school at the time, so it was only a year and a bit until she went to high school. We felt if home education didn't work out, we could always just put her back into school and start afresh as if she'd never left. However, I was hoping secretly that she wouldn't want to go back.

Indie, on the other hand, was always a little bit away with the fairies, and she still is. Any teacher that has taught Indie needs a certificate of attendance and a stiff drink! Not long before we took her and Poppy out of school, I got called in to see Indie's teachers. They told me that she was very good at her work if they were with her all the time, encouraging her, but as soon as they left her, she kinda gave up. They showed me her book where she had been writing in one direction one day and had then decided to flip the book on its head and write in the other direction the next day. Typical Indie and actually it's what I love most about her.

She is very whimsical and not the most enthusiastic when it comes to putting pen to paper. Hands on tasks she is amazing at, but her concentration in front of a workbook is zilch. After Idan and I talked about it, we decided that Indie would come out of school as well. Her laid back, whimsical nature had started to mellow, I could see that she was finding work utterly boring and was starting to cause a disruption in class, because being the class clown was fun.

Indie was also spending a lot of time out of school at hospital for random tests, sometimes for days at a time, and this was another reason for thinking that home education was probably a good idea for both girls.

Before I was a home-ed mum, I was obviously a school-run mum. I was one of the mums that the teachers didn't really like. I thought I was freaking awesome, but I'd always turn up late, skip parents' evening and forget PE kits. Some days it would be a triumph if I actually got the kids there in one piece.

Dress-up days or non-uniform days were a walk in the park for me - as long as my friends sent me a text message the night before reminding me. I might have been shit at remembering when the play was, but I could turn my kid into the best bloody mouse ever for the nativity.

I think the worst 'terrible mum' moment was when I dropped Poppy off in reception, while chatting away to a friend without a care in the world. We were bitching about something and carried on all the way back to the car, where I finally realised I'd left two-year-old Indie in the classroom with the other kids. I had to do this terrible run of shame back into the classroom and pick up my toddler, who was looking completely bewildered, sitting on the carpet with the other kids taking the register. Luckily for me Poppy's teacher then was a legend and didn't make the feeling of the world swallowing me whole any worse. I'll always be grateful.

Despite being not much good at being a school-run mum, I always wanted to be a mum. I didn't realise it would be quite so early on, but you have to go with the flow and that was my flow. I met Idan when I was working at a local working farm which opened to the public. My main job was to please the public by doing demonstrations on farming-related things, everything from lambing to collecting eggs, and I loved that job - it was the only job I didn't find a chore and I had stuck at it since leaving college.

Never did I imagine at 18 I'd fall head over heels for an Israeli man, more than double my age, who totally swept me off my feet. It wasn't love at first sight, actually it was far from it I think we were just best friends, but fast forward a few years, which included a massive wedding where I became Mrs Hannah Whyman-Naveh, a job change and, after some rather distressing miscarriages, I was 20 and holding a brand-new baby. Poppy was born and she was adorable. She was everything I'd ever dreamed of, in a little bundle of newness and she loved her fucking dad! Yep, she cried for him, she adored him, I was just a bloody carrier pigeon. Two years and one month later and my adorable Indie Rose was born. A tiny little dot of a baby who was poorly from the start, so she quickly became an utter mummy's girl, naturally I adored every minute of it, although it was draining.

We've always been such a good team, all of us. Idan is away a lot as he is actually an engineer, so me and the girls spend a lot of time together and I make sure we fill that time up. In 2017, aged 48 and 29, Idan and I added Piper to the team, and she completed our family. She's a little monster now, but I can't remember life without her. She was the cherry on top of the most wonderful cake.

More recently we had the decision to make about Piper, who is obviously much younger and has never been to school. I have been really worried about us teaching her all the basics, like reading, writing, blooming phonics and 'sounding out'. Scares me shit-less, but I am confident she will learn as she is taking an interest already. We have decided to keep her home schooled, meaning Piper will never actually set foot in a proper mainstream school. She has been to nursery though, for my sanity and hers!

There's no right or wrong answer. The reasons why you want to home educate are yours and yours alone. No one should make you feel stupid or strange for wanting to home educate, it is a wonderful life. After all, why not home education? That would be my answer to the question.

What is home education?

What is
home
education?

What is home education?

Bear with me now, because the realm of home education is very varied. The home ed scale has very scheduled, school-like educators at one end, who are generally referred to as 'home-schoolers'. They follow a curriculum and set up their day/learning/ home very much like a school. At the other end you get the radical 'un-schoolers' who apply no form of structure at all and don't follow a curriculum. They're very child-led and don't believe in forced learning. In the middle you get people like me, who are winging it but with some rules.

My girls don't follow the national curriculum,

but I do make a note of what they should be learning each year. It is tempting at times to ask Siri if he has a teaching function, just to make my life a tad easier, but I'm better than that – I ask Alexa instead. I'm sure Alexa is on the verge of ringing ChildLine, what with the shouting, profanities and the constant asking of things I don't (but should) know. For example, within the space of ten minutes we could have:

Piper: "Alexa, play that song again"
Alexa: 'Do your ears hang low? Do they wobble to and fro? Can you tie 'em in a knot? Can you tie 'em in a...'
Me - *thinking for fuck sake:* "ALEXA SHUT UP! Piper turn that off!! Alexa, what year did the Titanic sink?"

Around all of that you get everyone else who just does it the way they feel like it. The main thing is that your child is learning, then you are fulfilling your role as a home educator. By law, the parent is responsible for making sure their child gets a full-time education once they turn 5 years old. Whether that is at home or in school is entirely up to the parent. Obviously, there are occasions when the local authority will step in, for example if your child has special needs, has been expelled from school or social services are involved. However, I am going to concentrate on those of us who have electively selected to home educate, as that is all I have experience of.

By now you're probably saying to yourself, "Oh bugger, I am not going to be one of those military-structured home edders, and I am definitely not going to be one of those kale eating, tie-dye loving, un-schoolers either. I just want to be normal." Well, I'm here to tell you I have learnt home ed doesn't judge, everyone is different. There is no box to fit into, it is basically whatever works for you.

If your brain is currently full of all the stereotypical visions of home-educated kids, then you'll resemble me when the idea popped into my head. I had this preconception that I'd have to stop farming, turn vegan and refuse to wear shoes. Or worse, turn into something that loosely resembles The Handmaid's Tale, but without the handmaids – praise be! The thought made me want to run for the hills - boarding school anyone? I wondered if there were people in the world of home ed that weren't on this scale. I spoke to a non-home edding friend, who reminded me that home education had moved on, meaning they didn't all breastfeed their children until they were 10, or make them recite the Bible. It encouraged me to find out a bit more and not just give up at the first hurdle like I had in the past.

I'm one of those wacky people that has probably tried most strange things in my 32 years on Earth (bar drugs and anything illegal, honest!). I have been a Goth in my teens with hair of all colours, mainly black. I then went to back to being the total opposite: an earthy blonde, organic and nature loving, banging on about anything farming. Now I've added 'eco-friendly' to the mix. I do sound like some hippy, but I really am normal (whatever normal is!).

I've done an array of jobs too. I've stacked shelves in the local shop, worked as a nursing auxiliary, worked in dog kennels and even went to college in 2016, while pregnant, to become a dog groomer. I hated every minute of all of them: stacking shelves gave me a wage but was so boring, patients require a level of patience that I just don't have, so nursing auxiliary wasn't my vocation, and dog grooming would have been ok if I didn't have to talk to the owners.

The only job I really ever loved, and didn't mind doing day in, day out, was farming. I have never been a fan of travelling around the world, I don't see the point when I have all I want here, but I am spontaneous. I have been known to drop everything to pick up a dog in Scotland or collect a pony from Cornwall. I see everything as an adventure, and I don't like to put too many obstacles in the way. My motto is, why not? No point regretting that you didn't give it a go – and that seemed to apply to home ed.

When I first started home educating, I went out and I bought loads of workbooks and more pencils and pens than WHSmith's. I tried to set up a school in my home by painting a massive chalkboard on one wall in our hall and making a 'school area'. That lasted all of about six weeks until the workbooks went, the chalkboard got painted over and we ended up doing lapbooks and projects on the dining room table.

We learnt very quickly what works for our family and what worked for each individual girl. I like being smack bang in between the un-schoolers and the structured home edders, which just means that we are doing it our way and, by doing it our way, we're doing it right. Saying that though, I do keep writing out a schedule (which gets ignored!) and I am rather tempted with dreadlocks, should I be worried?

Just remember home education is not school, that's the point. I was told to look at a typical school day: there is endless movement from one class to another, plus breaks and assemblies. There are usually some kids disrupting the class and lots of other random things going on. When you break that down, you notice that the time kids actually spend learning at school is very short, approximately three to four hours at the most. In which case, children do not need to be at a desk for six hours a day when they are home educated. The sheer fact that they're at home means it is more intense, and their time spent learning can be condensed. The average teacher has roughly 30 kids in their class, whereas you won't. Your children will have your undivided attention.

I am no teacher, I see myself only as a facilitator. I facilitate my child's learning. I give them the tools and the ability to learn. I do not need to be a rocket scientist, I am only expected to get them to GCSE level, not to teach them to fly to the moon. If they seriously want to fly to the moon, I can just tailor their learning towards this where possible. Take the time to find out what works for your family and don't be influenced by anyone else.

Once you get over the initial shock of every person you meet looking at your kids and saying "day off today?" or "is it the holidays for you?", you'll understand home education is extremely rewarding and you'll become very protective of your new lifestyle.

How do
I start?

How do I start?

"Like, oh my God, am I really doing this?"

This is exactly what I was thinking up until the day my children were officially deregistered from school. Deregistering is where your child is taken off the official school register and electively educated at home. It is then your job to make sure your child receives a full-time education in one way or another, and this can be via tutors/completely online or done solely by you. As we now know, there are several ways of home educating.

It's time to talk about The Letter. I'll do this

from my experience and what I have learnt (I do believe Scotland and Nothern Ireland are slightly different, so best to check with your local authority if you are unsure). This letter is probably the most important thing at the beginning of any home ed journey. It officially deregisters your child from the school system, and I was told to make sure the school actually received it (a copy of the template I used for this letter can be found on the Home Education UK Facebook page). Some people e-mail it across, some send it recorded, others just hand it into the office, and then some people will do all three. I just handed mine in.

I was then asked into the head teacher's office, which sounds alarming, but it was his job to encourage me to keep my children in school. As I was already 100% that home education was right for my children, not much mind changing took place. The school then sent a letter to the council to let them know I had deregistered my children. Shortly after this, I received a welcoming letter from the home education department of my local council, accepting my children and letting me know who my educational consultant was.

Along with this welcome letter was a massive form, which you can obviously fill in, but I just sent them a lovely letter back explaining what I intended to do with my girls and that I didn't need a home visit, also known as my educational philosophy. An educational philosophy is basically a statement of how your intend to teach your children and what you intend to teach your children. This normally satisfies most local authorities and it definitely did for mine. It's very common on Facebook groups for them to recommend that you stay arms' length from your local authority, but I find this is a regional matter and it really depends on who your educational consultant is, and whether you feel you are supported by them. I personally like to keep them in the loop, so I know where they are if I need them. I do understand though that not everyone has had the same experience. I just make sure I reply to anything they send me and always keep a record.

For those of you like me, with a child that hasn't actually started school, I would suggest you wait until the letter comes that asks you to choose your preferred school. I intend on replying back with a nice letter to explain that Piper will actually be home educated, along with her older sisters. Obviously, things do change year-on-year, so it is best to ask/research at the time, rather than just ignore things. I have been told to ignore letters in the past by other home edders, but in my personal opinion, ignoring things gets you no where. As long as you let them know that you are home educating that should be the only thing that you will need to do. Again, I will always keep my local authority updated with Piper's progress, when they ask, or when I feel the need.

Even though it is not currently a legal requirement, I do keep all the work the girls do, within reason. I blog our life on Facebook and my website, so most of our outings are documented there, but any work they do on paper, I make sure it is kept in either a book or a folder. I'll explain about lapbooks later on, but they're a great way of condensing down a whole project's work and can be stored in a box folder easily. This way you can send your local authority samples of your children's work if they ask for it. Another thing that is useful is a tutor report, if you use a tutor then getting them to write a small report on your child's progress will be sufficent. From when I researched all this, I found that the local authorities tend to only contact you once a year, just to see how you are doing., and will only step in if they feel a full-time education is not being met for your child.

How much does it cost?

How much does it cost?

Only you know if you can afford home ed. As the saying goes, 'no one can ever afford kids', well to me, no one can ever really afford home ed. You just learn to adapt.

There are pros and cons when it comes to the cost of this life. I won't have school lunches to pay for, or buses, or uniform. I won't have trips and the 'voluntary' contribution for transport, which is never actually voluntary. Instead, I have endless trips to the fridge to fork out for, a constant flow of new leggings and tops, books galore and money for tutors and exams, if I choose to go down that route. There is still the cost of pens and pencils, like at school, and possibly workbooks if that is your thing. So it can get costly but, in my opinion, the cost of school vs home ed is much of a much-ness.

I guess the main factor of home education is the parents' working status. Idan is the main earner and he has a solid job, even though he's self-employed. I am the stay-at-home mum, first and foremost, but I do run a side-line illustration business that gets stressful at times. I juggle things by doing my job in the evening when the kids are in bed or when their dad is home to entertain them. So, if you work from home anyway, great.

I know several working parents, though, that manage to home educate. They work different shift patterns so while one is at home the other is at work and vice versa. Single working parents must struggle more, but I guess they rely on childminders or grandparents, even the other parent, if they're still in the picture. Whatever the case, home education is doable, you don't have to give up work to do it though it's definitely easier.

What does matter is having both parents on board, and it helps if family members get on board too. Home educating your child is about putting their best interests at the forefront, and definitely not because it's an easy life or to get handouts because trust me, it isn't and there aren't any. At least none that I've heard of and if this changes I wish to be the first to know about it!

When I first mentioned to Idan about wanting to home educate he was shocked. His response was "What? Don't be stupid, woman? Why would you want to do that?" You may want to read that in your best Israeli accent just to get the full effect. Whenever I piss my husband off, he tends to go up five octaves and revert back to the mid 90s on his kibbutz. It is inaudible to some, but I am fluent.

He soon came round to the idea, however, and actually is now more confident and forceful about it than me at times. He did have a bit of a blip during lockdown number one, but I think that was more his tension about not working than it was about home educating. Lockdown was/is a totally different thing and something that we all struggled with, home educated or not.

I didn't have that much of a hard time trying to convince my family. My parents were a bit worried about how I would cope and if I would ever get a break, but otherwise they were really supportive. They were intrigued by home ed and somewhat excited by the concept.

I've read on home ed Facebook groups that many people do have a hard time with getting their family to accept their choice to home educate. I imagine that must be quite hard and the only bit of advice I can give you is to sit down with them and discuss it without arguing.

This is a decision for the whole family, so you have to be a team. You can obviously explain your reasons and why you are so passionate about home education. I actually showed some YouTube clips to my family, which really helped. There was one in particular which was a rap about the school system called What is school for? by Prince Ea. The video is great, I don't know much about the rapper, but a lot of what he says in the video is spot on. Worth a watch.

One thing in your favour is schools aren't going anywhere. If it doesn't work out for you and your family, you can always return your children to school.

Encouraging learning

Encouraging learning

So, how do you get your child to work? This is a tricky one, and one of the things that a lot of mums ask me when it comes to home education.

Let me take you back to the beginning of our journey. When we started, we were full of good ideas: we wanted to replicate school at home with our big chalkboard and workbooks and God knows how many pens and pencils. Right from the start we could see it really wasn't going to work. My girls were more inclined to work when they were doing a project or an experiment, or something more hands on.

It was decided to give them a break and give us a chance to work out what we really wanted to do. We took a week's holiday at home, we didn't go anywhere, and before I knew it the girls were actually asking to work. Not actually asking to sit down with a workbook or do a spelling test, but they were asking questions and that gave me a brilliant idea. Every time my girls asked a question, we would learn all about the answer.

For example, if Indie woke up one morning and asked why the sky is blue, we would research it by watching documentaries, reading books and scouring the internet. Then we would make a lapbook (I'll explain these later) of what we'd learned, as well as recording the weather. From that another question came along, like what is a tornado? Before I knew it, the girls were learning, and it was all happening naturally, I wasn't having to force anything and there wasn't a workbook in sight. This probably sounds very 'unschooling' of me, but I promise I do try to keep it quite structured by keeping a diary of topics and ideas of things to come up with, but if they ask a question then I just go with it.

To give you an idea, this is a typical Whyman-Naveh day:

The day starts with feeding all the animals. They get fed before anyone else. If Idan is home, he and Indie will go outside to feed the chickens, sheep, outside dogs and horses, while I get Piper up - and fight with her for an hour about what she's wearing. If Idan isn't home, Indie and I take it in turns to go outside and feed the animals. Poppy will go downstairs to do the dogs and 'tidy' the kitchen. Once outside is finished, we come in and have breakfast. This is super important, my girls and Idan LOVE breakfast and, Christ, they can eat first thing in the morning. It consists of eggs, salad, bread and olives. Weird right? Don't ask.

After breakfast we decide what we are doing for the day, this could be a subject or project chosen by the girls, or a certain job on the farm (like trimming sheep feet or building a chicken house), basically anything. In lockdown we were quite restricted, but normally this could mean a day out, depending on the topic. If the girls have work to do like English homework or some of their coursework, then this will get done first. On a Thursday the girls do an English online class with a tutor and after that they have work to finish before the next lesson, so Thursdays are normally full up.

After lunch we do a bit more work before mucking out the ponies. Poppy will do the dogs' kennels and normally do some training. Indie or Piper may ride too, depending on the weather. After the ponies are put to bed we go inside and clear up ready for dinner. We all muck in for dinner, even Piper. The girls always lay the table and make drinks.

After dinner is their free time. They can call

friends, play games and just relax, that's if there are no clubs on or friends' houses to visit.

This happens every day of the week, we don't have days off as such, like at a weekend or half term, we just roll with it. We do have 'off days' though and that is ok, some days we accomplish nothing more than watching endless reruns of The Vicar of Dibley – I class that as R.E.

I'm not sure how this looks on paper, but some days it seems very little to us and other days we feel like we've done loads, it just depends on what we are learning and what we are doing. Some mornings we could be watching documentaries about a chosen topic, but other days we could be visiting a museum on another topic, it's crazy fun!

I do make sure they attend their Zoom meeting on a Thursday with their online English tutor. We're actually looking for a maths tutor at the moment, hopefully by the time this book goes out we will have found one that doesn't cost me a kidney. It's only been the last six months that we have used a tutor, purely to make sure that they were interacting with other children during lockdown and they love it so much that we've carried it on. Win win.

Poppy and Indie also do online courses as an extra. Poppy is doing an IGCSE course in double science and Indie is doing an equine course. Both of which they chose, so we don't really have to push them to do it. As its online they can happily do it in their pyjamas if they have too!

If you intend on being more structured, I understand that this way of doing it probably won't work for you but I think kids like learning, they're little sponges for information, and I think they want to learn. As long as you are willing to adapt your way of facilitating that learning, then I don't think you will ever have a stale kid that doesn't want to learn. I think all children will need encouragement at times but if they're having fun, they will be more willing.

For those who are struggling, there are many curriculums out there on a range of werid and wonderful subjects, you just have to search for them. I have found curriculums entirely based around Harry Potter, for example. Theres one using Lego and even a curriculum for Minecraft lovers. You also get the curriculums that are based on nature and the great outdoors, or curriculums based on animals. There really is so much out there to help encourage children to work, engage with the topic and hopefully help the parent to facilitate their learning.

Another thing I'd like to add here is hobbies. If ever our lifestyle came into play, it is now. My girls will spend three or four hours doing projects/ work in a day but around that I encourage them to be outside with their animals. Indie is into her ponies and Poppy loves her sheep and dogs. Giving them something they're responsible for daily and something else to concentrate on gives them more to life than just home ed. I can teach so much when we are rambling out over fields on a dog walk or riding the ponies. There is a massive sence of freedom when on horseback and I love taking all the girls out, including Piper, with the ponies and dogs to explore the woods and beaches. We stop for picnics and escape from four walls. We discuss all sorts of things from nature to history. Actually, some of my best history lessons have been whilst on horse back. We play games along the way, especially with Piper, she will count the blue flowers or spot a certain bird. The older two like to explore new places, find new routes and go off the beaten track. We have a lovely river that runs through the meadow where we keep some sheep and horses. This river is sometimes shallow, if there at all, and sometimes it is full and deep. My girls love to visit this river and play in it regardless of the time of year. When it is shallow it is good for finding bugs, finding the natural spring, building dams and paddling. When it is deep, it is brilliant for taking the dogs swimming, for throwing in sticks and stones, making boats that hopefully float and for engineering new ways to get across it. All of this is a wonderful sense of adventure, from the riding, to the playing by the river and I am feeling withdrawal symptoms thanks to Covid and the current weather.

Poppy is due to start lambing soon, for the second time. Last year was a huge learning curve for her and she learnt a lot. She has grown up around lambing, after all, lambs were being bottle fed in the kitchen from the day Poppy was born, but there is a huge sense of responsibility for her these days. Biology is a big part of sheep farming and even mini farmers have to learn quickly about life and death, and how not to be squeemish over lamb-goo (as it is known), poop and placenta. I always had visions of making it 'big time' as a sheep farmer. Several times I had got very close, but life always seemed to have a way of changing the plan. I realised I was probably better off keeping it as a hobby and Poppy has now taken over the sheep and has her own little flock of Greyfaced Dartmoors, plus other waifs and strays.

Before we moved here, Idan and I ran a little smallholding with goats, chickens, sheep, cows and, most importantly, horses. Horses have been in my life since I was a child, and while I knew I never wanted to pursue them as a job, I was certain I would never be without one. I've always owned native ponies, I love showing them and turning them out to the best of my ability. However, in recent years I have become a Pony Club mum, driving the child and the pony to the event, hanging around fetching, carrying and taking photos, freezing my butt off in the process, only to take said child and pony back home to fumigate in hope of stopping the spread of mud and horse manure. But I'm glad my children love animals as much as me.

For those who aren't lucky enough to have animals, I would encourage you to pursue some hobbies with your kids. Doesn't matter what it is, it will only help with their learning in my opinion. Could be woodwork, or extreme Lego building (is that a thing?), coding or ballet. Just let them explore their interests and give them an escape. If your kids are like mine, they can become super passionate about hobbies when they find one they really like. These passions can then be put to good use and become jobs, if that's what they want, and they also provide learning opportunities.

Indie's main passion in life is riding horses. She wants to be a jockey and I will help her in any way necessary if that's what she wishes to do. We tailor all her learning towards horses now and it works. Maths can easily be learnt by making horses' feeds, things like half a scoop of this and 300 grams of that is maths without even thinking about it. Her writing has come on leaps and bounds since she's been doing the equine course and she also learns science.

Poppy is unsure what she wants to be as she gets older. At one time it was a baker, which was great because baking is an ideal way to learn maths and science, also English because reading a recipe is a big part of baking. She now thinks she wants to be an architect. She has several hobbies, mainly she enjoys dog agility, which is physical education and thinking on her feet. She also loves photography, which could be classed as art and science. Even Piper is learning when she counts the chicken eggs every day, for example.

There really is learning in everything the girls do and we encourage hands-on activities. Indie has recently laid a concrete floor in her tack room. Idan mixed the concrete and we let her put it down on the floor, a whole 12ft by 16ft. She enjoyed every minute of it! That may make us sound bizarre, but not many nine year olds can say they've laid a concrete floor.

What about exams?

What about exams?

Another thing I was worried about before home educating was exams. When Poppy was struggling at school, she was about to take her mock SATs. I was under the impression that all kids needed to sit their exams, including SATs or else they wouldn't get a job when they were older. As it turns out SATs are purely a test to see if the level of education at the school is adequate, basically to see if they are doing their job. They do show what level your child is at with their learning, but the main purpose is to make sure the teacher is teaching in a way that the child understands.

A few months before the girls left school, Poppy came home very upset saying she didn't understand fractions at all. I must admit I'd been super hands off with the girls' learning up until that point. I wasn't really a fan of homework and I didn't write down any of their reading. I was one of those mums that would do a mass reading record, using different pens so no one would notice, just so the girls passed a few of the goals for Readathon - utter nightmare.

Anyway, she was crying and really quite anxious because she had a test the next day and was worried she would be bottom of the class. I told her not to worry and that I would sit with her all night if I had to, until she understood fractions. In typical mum mode, I did the whole pizza method, where you have a pizza and cut in half and then half again is quarters and half a quarter is an eighth etc. I explained how to add them together and how to take away, using the pizza. She finally understood it and we were getting somewhere.

Next day came and she went off to school so happy, knowing she was going to do well on her test. I wasn't expecting what happened when I picked her up that afternoon. Both girls jumped into the car in the turning circle and Poppy was very subdued. I asked her how her test was and she just sobbed, it was heart breaking. When we got home, she explained that, as it was a mock SATs test, even though the answers were right, since she didn't show workings out the same way her teacher had showed them, it was in fact all wrong. I was livid. Fuming. This was the first time that leaving school even popped into my head and after that Poppy just ended up getting worse, so these thoughts ended up becoming actions.

I quickly found out that, depending on what your child wishes to do with their life, exams may be wanted but not necessarily needed. Here's where it starts to get technical; after researching, I found kids don't have to be in school to sit GCSEs. You can actually be an external student like a home ed student and sit IGCSEs in certain schools and colleges that allow it. You can also be any age, so if your child feels confident to sit a Maths GCSE at 12 then that's entirely up to them. They also don't have to sit all their IGCSEs all together.

IGCSEs are international GCSEs and are recognised outside the UK as well as in the UK. There are some differences, the main one being the IGCSE exam is usually longer, as the student does not submit coursework. One thing you do have to take into account is the cost. Home educated kids do not get things for free: you will have to pay for the exams and the use of the premises, and prices vary depending on the test centre and the exam board, so shop around.

Another route to the job your child wants would be college. Some colleges do 14-16 year old courses which usually put your child through their English and maths GCSE, as well as the course itself. This is quite popular with home educated students, but not all colleges run them. The simplest way is to start off on either a level 1 or 2 course at 16 like any other school leaver. Colleges will happily take home educated students as they are often better at time management and have work experience in their chosen subject.

As for universities, no home educated child should find universities problem. I did speak to a few people from Universities on this topic, who were exhibiting at our local County show, their reply was that if you meet the requirements, you are just like any other applicant.

So please don't think for one minute that a home educated child will not get far in life. If anything, they could get there more smoothly. I have been told work experience is worth more than it's given credit for, and since our children can tailor their life's worth of learning to their passion, it's worth thinking about. Can't do that at school. After all, home ed didn't do Thomas Edison and Teddy Roosevelt too bad.

Making friends
&
keeping friends

Making friends
&
Keeping friends

60

Making friends and keeping friends

Schooling isn't just about learning, of course. Having friends and socialising is an important part of the time children spend in education. Before the awful lockdowns, when life was normal, my girls had the best of both worlds. They were doing our home ed life during the day and then in the evenings they went clubs and they saw their friends. At weekends they would either meet friends for sleepovers or we would be out and about socialising. Back then, socialising was easy for home edders.

The myth that home ed children are socially awkward and don't socialise very often really annoys me. It was one of the things that shocked me the most, when I noticed that my children had actually come out of their shell once we started home ed. They would talk to anyone, especially people in shops who would say "oh have you got a day off school?" to which my girls would then go off on a tangent explaining that they are actually home educated. Most were really intrigued, but we got a few who were stuck up and would just roll their eyes.

Home ed kids get to choose their friends, which school children don't. School children are forced to sit in a classroom with other children that they may not even like. They may be like my Poppy, who felt completely isolated in her classroom, even though she was technically one of the 'popular ones'. My girls get to choose their friends now, regardless of ages or gender, and it really makes a difference.

Then lockdown hit. BOOM.

It has been quite a tough time, for everyone. This isn't a home ed issue; I think it's just a Covid issue and I am sure we will get back to how we were. We must.

We have adapted though. I asked on home ed Facebook groups and farming groups if there were any children that wanted to talk to other kids. So Poppy and Indie have made friends via FaceTime and WhatsApp, which means they can socialise even during lockdown.

Covid Lockdown schooling

I think it's worth saying a word about the home-schooling that has happened as a result of lockdowns – I'll say this now and I'll say it once, this lockdown schooling is shit. It is far from the home education I have come to know and love. It was driving me bonkers during the first lockdown when I saw all these mums that were trying to replicate school at home and they were like "oh, hash tag home education" with their Instagram-friendly photo. Bollox! It is not real. Not to mention, I will never be a mum with a crumb-free house and an Instagram-able face – I'm lucky if I can get a family photo without my kids pulling each other's hair or poking out a tongue.

The reasons I hate lockdown schooling are (like I have to explain!):

A) we are not hermits that don't ever go out of the house. That in itself is an insult to home edders. All of the home edders I've met are generally outgoing folk, who enjoy going to clubs and groups, and having the opportunity run around freely and climb trees.

B) we don't get handouts from schools to facilitate our children's learning. That kind of learning wouldn't work anyway and kind of defeats the object as to why most of us home educate. Wouldn't it be lovely if our local council was handing out all the resources that we needed to home educate our children, but unfortunately it is never going to happen, so the school doing exactly that is not home education. Plus, some of the timetables I have seen have been totally unrealistic. Again, thats not to say teachers are in the wrong, they too are struggling, I'm sure.

C) it gives a very unrealistic view of what my version of home ed is really like. I find more and more people saying that they couldn't do home ed, that I deserve a medal, all because they couldn't cope during lockdown. ARGH! It's not the same. That is probably the reason for this book in all honesty, to show my experience of home ed and how different it is from what school mums have experienced during this trying time.

Lockdown schooling was and is awful for everybody, especially those who would normally be working and/or were still having to work from home with children who are not normally at home. I can understand why people couldn't wait until their children went back to school and I wholeheartedly think that I would feel the same if I had been in their situation. I have friends who are tearing their hair out, not knowing whether they are coming or going and the worst bit is, I cannot offer any help. It is so far removed from what I do with my girls that whatever advice I give wouldn't help them.

If I'm totally honest, during the first lockdown we didn't really do much work, we just let the girls decide what they wanted to do. They did lots of riding and dog agility, at home obviously, and we used the time to do crafts and jobs around farm. We fully embraced lockdown life. Obviously, Daddy was home, so we made the most of that as well by watching lots of films and just having as much time together as possible in the hope that we would never have to be put in that situation again.

Someone once said to me after the first lockdown, "oh well, you must be used to this way of life, because you home educate". NO, we are fun, free and whimsical, just like Indie. We don't do locked up.

I am sure there are plenty of you reading this book who are planning on home educating due to the current state of the world. This pandemic is hideous, and I can understand the worry of sending a child to school fearing them getting the virus or even just bringing it home. My advice is not to view lockdown schooling as a trial run, as there is no trial run to home education. I say use whatever time they have off as a chance to get yourselves out of the "school" process, de-school you and the kids, and make a plan of action. If home education truly is for you, then this process will be easy, and you will move life around to accommodate it. Don't get hung up on curriculums and schedules, just chill out and write that de-reg letter!

If anything, lockdown has made me feel very lucky and more humbled about our set up and where we live. We are very lucky; it must be hard for those who aren't in a rural area and especially hard for those who live in flats, with no outside space. I cannot comment on that life, I have no experience of it, but I do feel for those who are completely locked up with children in this situation. Again, this is why I say normal home education is nothing like lockdown schooling. In normal times, you'd be able to leave the house and explore.

Groups and clubs

Groups and clubs

Setting aside the Covid situation, groups and clubs are great and there will be more than you think. Forest schools and farm schools seem to be cropping up all over the place and most cater for home ed kids during the week. These are great for the social element, both child and parent, but they're also good for getting outdoors and exploring.

To be honest, lot of these things are just not my cup of tea, but then we have a farm full of animals and trees, and my children ask a lot of interesting questions during a good old jolly through the woods. The groups I have been to saw me spend my time freezing my arse off while my kids ran around together, and I drank something I made myself at home. Pointless for me but for those who don't have woods, animals and nature on the doorstep it is a lifeline.

After-school clubs like Rainbows, beavers, guides, cubs and scouts and suchlike allow home ed kids and are normally fairly cheap. Parents also don't have to stay, which I think is a wonderful aspect. As my kids get older, I am noticing they need time away from me more and more and this is a good opportunity for that. Sign 'em up! It gives you a bloody break, too, if Dad is about. Open the wine early and let him do the pickup!

I have also mentioned Pony Club. Indie has been doing Pony Club for a couple of years now and not only does she learn to ride, she meets new friends and works towards qualifications. We are a proper Pony Club family – Piper will start this year – but if horses aren't your thing, I highly recommend getting your child into a club they love.

Our area has home ed groups which get together either weekly or monthly. They do organised trips or group experiences, which can be really good and great for socialisation. Everything from swimming to singing to skating goes on in our area, even beach trips. I have even found out they're doing some online Zoom clubs, which is great. If you don't have anything like this in your area, you could always start one up.

It is also worth ringing around all the local libraries, open farms, sea life centres, zoos, museums, anything remotely touristy that may offer a weekday discount for home edders. Best to ask: if you don't ask, you won't know.

Blips and
tough questions

Blips and tough questions

Let's face it, we're all going to have them; blips are part of daily life. We've had blips. I've had Poppy asking to go back to school during lockdown because she had no friends. We've soon rectified that, but it was horrible at the time to see her not happy. We explained that everyone was in the same boat but, to an 11 year old, not seeing friends is the end of the world. Indie went through a patch at the beginning where she would just stare at questions in a workbook and act dumb. She isn't dumb at all, but was stale and finding all the work a bit too much like brainwashing, so we changed the way we did things and it worked, thankfully. Now she writes endless amounts for her equine course without problem. At the time, though, it was really challenging. I did feel like I was hitting my head against a brick wall. Just a simple change and it was all sorted, so it really is trial and error.

Blips will come for parents as well. I personally haven't had one yet, but I know I could at some point. This life is not easy, it's a big responsibility and the feeling of 'am I doing this thing right?' can overwhelm you at times. I'm a pig-headed old cow, though, so my stubbornness wouldn't let me give in. I believe in this way of life now and I know it's right for my girls. However, schools are still there if shit seriously does hit the fan - all my girls could go back, no harm done. Just because this life works now, doesn't mean it always will.

Probably my biggest issue, if I was to say I had one, is wondering what would happen if anything happened to Idan, for example he left, or lost his job, or even died. I'd have to go back to work and then the girls would most likely have to go back to school. I know if I died, they'd be back to school in a flash, regardless of how much he supports this way of life. If it meant him actually having to do some of that educating, then it would be over faster than you can say 'new wife, please'.

A lot of women manage to home educate and work full or part time, but I'm not sure if I'd want to do that. I would give it a try, again through pig-headedness more than anything, but I run a small business that I started myself during lockdown and even that is hard work around home ed, doable but hard work. It's a case of juggling and just hoping you don't drop any balls!

Anyway, talking of blips, now I am a home ed mama, where is this Zen I was promised? I know the thigh gap was a big ask but I wouldn't mind being more 'downward dog', which would probably make me a better parent right? More relaxed. Less muttering "shut the fuck up" under my breath in the direction of my husband.

Sex ed and other cringy topics

As your child gets older, they will start asking some random questions. When they're at school they find out most of their queries from other kids, meaning it's normally wrong or, umm, muddled. They do need this in my opinion, hence why I feel friends are important for my girls. With friends they can discuss anything and have a giggle about it, the kind of stuff you just don't ask your parents. School kids also have sex education lessons but, if I remember rightly, this was mainly spent watching weird videos and cringing, while trying not to make eye contact with the opposite sex. I was still none the wiser why I was putting a condom onto a toilet roll holder, but I did know it was probably an important aspect.

I've always been very open with my girls. My mum was NOT open with me. She thought she was but in fact she made everything into a fairy-tale. She even cried when I started my period - I didn't know whether to be proud or scared of impending death!

I answer any question as truthfully as possible and I don't get awkward about it. I'm not sure if it's years of farming that has made me this way, maybe. I have no problem talking about covering, tupping or whether its "poo is a bit too runny for my liking", with anyone who will listen. It's all very normal here and I guess that makes topics like this a little easier. I can always compare to some kind of animal.

Take, for example, how babies are made: "Well, a man and a woman do exactly what Spartacus does to the ewes, only men are just allowed to have one girlfriend at a time. Once they have tupped, the man's sperm travels up the lady's vajayjay and into one of her eggs. This turns into a baby." BISH BASH BOSH. I mean, you don't need to be too graphic, but honesty really is the best policy if you ask me.

There are also some fabulous books out there for anyone who is struggling. I highly recommend them if you have daughters like me, because periods will be something you discuss and books related to female puberty are brilliant for this. They just confirm what you already tell them, after all, us parents don't know much. I will put the name of the book we have in the resources page in case you are interested.

Keeping your sanity

Keeping your sanity

I keep referring to home ed mothers, but actually a lot of dads do take on this role. Obviously, I am a mum so I'm speaking from my experience only when it comes to keeping sanity when we home educate.

Firstly I just want to say that home education is not like having your children home during school holidays. When my children were at school, they did all their learning at school and then came home for some downtime, especially school holidays. I'd let them play all day long and any structure went out the window. When I worked, I just spent most of the time worrying about where my children were going to be.

Now we home educate, life is a lot different. Learning is done at home, it's more relaxed and my kids get to play more and have more downtime, so the need for an actual holiday from 'schoolwork' goes away. Home ed learning is fun; even if you're the most scheduled parent and the work is a bit more intense, your child still gets more downtime than a schooled child. What I'm trying to say is children aren't coming home on a school holiday and acting feral, because they are home all the time anyway. I ended up finding some kind of routine and the kids settled into home ed life.

When my kids had established this routine and were happy, I found that home ed life just became normal. It's very hard to explain, but in my experience home ed kids like to keep themselves busy and they won't be under your feet all the time.

When it comes to regaining some sanity – because I'm not going to sit here and pretend that home education is not hard for the parent - I would make sure that you do have people around you that are willing to help. Gone are the days of nice breakfasts in a café with Idan looking lovingly into my eyes, while we pretend we have no responsibilities. These days a breakfast out consists of a Maccy D's bacon bagel and a Tropicana.

Luckily for me, my husband is around for roughly four days during the week. He notices now if I need to have an afternoon to myself to work, or just have a bath and watch a movie, for which I am so unbelievably grateful (she says, as her toddler walks in with a copper pipe stuck on her thumb, that her husband just casually left on the coffee table - thanks Idan!).

Sometimes we just need to remind ourselves that we are more than just a mum and even the smallest things can do that. For me, it's driving in my car with music blaring and singing at the top of my voice, or having an evening to myself to go and groom my horse without constant "Mum, Mum, Mum". Maybe I'll ride my horse at some point this year − feeling strangely optimistic, but hey I am a glutton for punishment.

This is obviously a mum thing more than a home ed thing, but either way we all need a break and more so when your children are with you all the time. It is good if you have grandparents as well that can help especially if you are a single parent and working around home educating. My parents had me much older than most other parents. They used to look after Poppy for me every weekend, so I could go to work, but when Indie came along I gave up working and my parents have had their own issues, so even though they live right next door to me, they don't have my children as often as some of my friends' parents do. Idan and I do manage to get a night away once a year, but that is it. We don't really mind; we like being here and we have the animals.

It just makes the times that we do get away together even more special.

Idan works away a lot so he'd rather be at home. Idan's love of all things Alaska has got a tad out of hand, though, he is insisting that we will all move there one day – Otto and Eivin has a lot to answer for (if you know, you know). He would never last out in Alaska, he wears a coat while the heating comes on and he shivers when opening the fridge. I'm sure it's just because he wants a Discovery Channel deal, so he gets loads of new machinery chucked in and can do a whole programme dedicated to him using them. I keep explaining that the only Discovery deal he will get is the one Land Rover gives him when we upgrade our car. Still, he won't give up on the Alaska life.

Another thing we do, when we are not in lockdown, is a family holiday to Bluestone in Wales each year. We absolutely love it there. I am sure there are much more glamorous places but for some reason this holiday just suits our family. The kids love it, I love it and Idan loves it (nearest thing to Alaska he's ever going to get). Outdoors for a week in a lovely log cabin in Pembrokeshire, doing all outdoorsy stuff, right up our street! It is like Center Parcs but without the massive price tag. There is so much on offer, even a spa. This holiday really gives me something to look forward to each year and somehow that just seems to be enough. Plus, we don't have to ask for permission to take the kids out of school on holiday. GET IN!

They say that you don't really need to take a break from something that you love and while I agree, I do think we all need a break from the norm at times. The home ed life is a beautiful life and one I would encourage, but before you start this journey just make sure there are people around you who are willing to help and can notice when you need a break.

Outside of lockdown life, I do love to get my lashes done and I have a hairdresser come to the house. Both make me feel more feminine and less like a homeless person. The way I see it is, I hardly drink, other than huge amounts of tea, and I don't smoke, nor I am one to take extravagant holidays, so if it makes me look and feel less like the Gruffalo it's worth the money.

Project
Ideas

Project
Ideas

Project ideas

Oh, I do love a project! My girls and I have become very fond of lapbooks over the past 18 months. Some need a decent level of tea installed before attempting, purely because they're so boring, but the majority are pretty cool. I soon realised just how dunce I actually was. Obviously, I didn't show the kids this revelation, but during our bee project I spent a good 80% of it with my mouth open, in total awe. Who knew bees were so God damned interesting, it definitely made me think twice before I swat whatever is buzzing around my head in the summer! I found myself putting bee drinking stations out instead and planting bee-loving plants - which I quickly regretted putting so close to the house.

So, I am going to show you how we make them. Lapbooks are great for storing work (they fold up), good for going back over work the kids have learnt and for helping it actually 'sink in'. Plus, they're fun for the kids.

Read closely or you may miss it (sarcasm at its finest).

1) Get an A3 piece of coloured card

2) Gently fold the card in half down the long side but don't make a fold, just mark where the centre is.

3) Flatten the card out

4) Pull the edges of the card into the middle to meet the centre mark.

5)Fold each side to make two flaps.

6)That's it!

You now have an A4 size piece of card which resembles a spa brochure (we live in hope) with an opening at the front. You can cover all of this card with what they (you) learn during your project. I have found incorporating these sensory elements into my girl's work really does help with their concentration. The topic we are learning seems to be remembered easier when making lapbooks and they look forward to doing them, purely because of the hands-on-craft part. Sounds utterly ludicrous right, well bear with me, they work so I urge you to give them a try.

I asked my girls to list a few projects which they really enjoyed, and both said the bee project, World War II, weather and horses. World War II is quite self-explanatory, it was more of a history lesson really, with some work sheets and a timeline chucked in. We learnt about evacuees being sent to the country and concentration camps, which Idan was able to help with as he visited one in the past.

The bee project was pretty fabulous, I printed off a few worksheets from Twinkl, which explained each part of the bee and what it's called. I also looked on Pinterest for some inspiration and, as usual, Pinterest saved the day with such good ideas. We made some bee houses, planted the regrettable plants and watched some amazing YouTube clips on what bees actually do. All in all, this took us almost a week to do the whole project and lapbook and what I loved the most was the fact they wanted more.

The weather project was one of the first projects we ever did. At this point we weren't doing lapbooks, they just wrote on paper and put it in a folder, so we did eventually go back and make the project into several lapbooks. The weather project ended up being massive. At first it was just weather in general. We learnt what weather was, using YouTube and Twinkl worksheets. We recorded the weather for a week by making a weathervane, rain collector and also Bubba's barometer and temperature gauge.

Then we looked into different types of weather. Indie asked what a tornado was and, thanks to

Pinterest, they showed us how to make a tornado in a jar from everyday things found in the kitchen (see the jar on the title page). We learnt all about erosion and how weather affects the world and from there we went onto global warming. That then took us to the environment, palm oil and recycling.

Madness isn't it, but an amazing kind of madness. Even putting this down on paper seems bonkers, but this is our life now and when I see it in black and white, I realise how amazing it actually is. I may even give myself a pat on the back at this point.

For the horse project (I wonder who chose that?) we did anatomy, points of the horse, feeding, husbandry, poisonous plants, even teeth. Obviously, horses are easy for us, but you could do dogs, cats, hamsters, any animals really, even dinosaurs. Saying that, you could still do horses if you found a good riding school or yard willing to help. We did this project before lockdown, so we took a trip to the National History Museum, to take a look at the evolution of the horse, amongst other things. I am hoping we will be able to go again one day soon when Covid buggers off. Anyway, that then sparked a project on the ocean and things like sharks and whales. I guess you see the pattern emerging.

This is what I mean when I say one question leads another and, before you know it, you learn so much without even realising it. Ok, my girls don't sit at a table doing times tables and spellings, and maybe there is an argument that they should, but they're still learning both in a roundabout way. Measuring rain is still maths, deducting yesterday's rain from today's, well that's pretty useful. I am 32 and I still use my fingers for counting at times, and I definitely sound things out. WED-NES-DAY, there's one!

Phew, I got here finally. I hope you have enjoyed hearing about my home ed randomness. I do hope it's been insightful and that home ed is now slightly less daunting, knowing I do it and I cope.

I do love home education, as I am sure you can see, and even though being a parent is hard and home ed makes things even harder, it doesn't have to be a tear-your-hair-out situation. It can be very rewarding and very humbling, and you get to spend all your time with the most amazing creations in the world. I personally wouldn't change it for all the tea in china, and that's a lot of tea.

Resources

Resources

Resources

Twinkl - I use Twinkl at least once a week. It is well worth the subscription. Brilliant for downloading everything from whole topics, to headed paper, to colouring pages, to work sheets. They list everything in year groups, even early years. If you are doing a project or finding out about something in particular, have a look on Twinkl, they'll have something related to it.

Home Education UK Facebook page - An utter lifeline for home ed mamas. You can ask pretty much anything without judgement. There are some long-standing home edders on there, with a wealth of knowledge. They also have a brilliant template of the deregistration letter, written by one of the group members.

Reading eggs - A brilliant reading game for two to 13 year olds. Just sign up and download the app. It helps with phonics, vocabulary and much more.

Toucan boxes - Not cheap, but I had them for Piper. It's a box subscription which send two crafts of your choice through the post. I only got the subscription for Piper due to the price, but it was well worth it. They do several different boxes for a range of ages and interests.

BBC bitesize - Helpful during lockdown, they had a lot on offer. Good resource for kids from KS1 all the way up to GCSE level.

YouTube and Netflix- Far too much for me to list but these platforms are amazing. There is so much to learn from Netflix documentaries and educational YouTube channels. All you have to do is search for the subject, that easy!

CPG books - Work books which are commonly used in schools. They cater for all core subjects from KS1 to A-level. We used these books when we first started out, but now we just incorperate them as and when we need too. Good quality books and easily purchased.

Ed Place - another good, paid home education app, with interactive worksheets in the core subjects. If you sign up, they will also send you progress reports for each child.

Pen pals - not exactly a resource, but still a very good way of encouraging written work. Find them a pen pal through a home ed page and get them writing letters!

Wild Math curriculum - A helpful little maths curriculum, based outside in nature. Very sweet and can be purchased for several different ages/levels.

"What's happening to me?" – By Usborne books. - A helpful book I bought Poppy to explain all the awkward stuff.

My home ed must haves

As I have come to find, my version of home education is a case of winging it and finding out what works for my family, but being set up correctly does help. I'm not saying you must have 100 pens, 3000 textbooks, 5 tutors and a chalkboard wall like we did, but there are somethings that help you along the way.

My main 'must-have' is a printer, and it needs to be a printer with cheaper ink because trust me, you'll be printing a lot. We have opted for the Epson EcoTank, purely for this reason.

Next on the list is the Twinkl subscription. For projects, Twinkl is indispensable. It has endless work sheets and information for so many different ages and stages, plus several topics. I can easily find Piper a colouring page or little game to do, or even Origami.

Folders are also well needed here. Box folders in particular for our lapbooks, and normal file folders for odd pieces of paper or odd worksheets. My kids have fun jazzing them up with stickers, which makes use of a rainy afternoon. We also have some exercise books, mainly sketch books. My girls love exercise books because they can write stories, create drawings or just make lists of things that pop into their minds. A very random thing, but one I must mention, is season tickets. I never bought season tickets before

I started home edding, I didn't feel the want or need. However, I soon learnt when I took on this life that we would be spending out a fortune on farm parks and other places, so season tickets would be a helpful saving. I have found however, that it is good to wait for the companies to have season ticket sales/promotions. Our two local places sell their family season tickets off half price at the beginning of each year. I make full use of that offer, which gives me a full year of entry for a one-off discounted price. As I have said before, it is worth asking around to see if your normal activity places offer discount for home ed families. After all, you bring them custom during the term times, which are normally quiet.

Learning to relax a lot and not take the mediocre things too seriously has helped me when home educating. There are times when I am pulling my hair out, when my girls just want to argue and I'm sat worrying if I am doing enough. This is when my season tickets really earn their keep. I take the girls out, let them run off steam, while I sit and have 5 minutes to reflect. Even when I cannot escape the house, I just have to take a step back, down tools, reset and not worry about the things which are out of my control.

Another must have is my car or a reliable mode of transport. Knowing I can get out and about is a necessity for me when home educating. If you are lucky enough to live in an area which has everything you need locally, then obviously you can walk or bike.

I don't have that, so I need my car, in order to get my kids out of the house and not get overwhelmed by four walls - like the majority of mamas right now in lockdown.

About me

About me

I love tea and cake, dogs and horses.
My girls are my world and everything I do is for them.

I wouldn't class myself as a writer. I wouldn't class myself as anything fancy in all honesty. I have recently become an illustrator, which I am very proud of, but even that was thrust upon me out of thin air. I now have a series of children's books out in the world and I illustrate for other people. Sounds utterly bonkers, when not even a year ago I hadn't picked up a pencil since my doss year at college, and I certainly hadn't the foggiest about writing a book.

When I think of being an author, I imagine myself as Jo from Little Women, sitting on a bare wooden floor in candlelight, with a long flowing dress and beautiful blonde hair, while I scribe away in ink. Well, that's far from reality. I'm currently typing this while shoving cottage pie in my mouth standing up, leant over the printer, plugged in so my MacBook doesn't run out of juice! The kids are watching Gnomeo and Juliet, so I can't even use dictate because it picks up the Gnome voices *eye roll*.

I'm a mama of three beautiful girls, a wife, a lover of all things with four legs and an utterly bonkers person that decided to home educate her children. I write a blog called Home Ed and Four Legs on Facebook and I decided it might make a good book too (it may also make a bad book and I may get a load of angry home ed parents in my inbox). Putting that aside, I just hope this book will give some idea of how home education works, from my perspective, and a laugh at the funny side of parenthood. We all need to laugh about it, or else we would just sit rocking.

Home education is the most amazing thing, but it is only what you make it. If you are set up correctly, in your mind, right from the start, then not only is it easier, but it is so rewarding. I don't know if this book will need updating in ten years time, things may have changed by then and I may sit there thinking I need to change that, or I need to update that. I don't know, because I am learning on the job, like all the other home ed mamas before me. What I do know is, whatever happens will be in the best interests of my children, I will continue adapt my approach to this life to suit each child and I will continue to make this journey one they will rememeber forever.

Our life is an utter mess, but it's a beautiful mess. It is a mess of happiness.

From my girls:

In many of these types of books, the opinion and experiences are always from the parent. So, I thought I would give my girls a chance to have their say on home education. This has been written down exactly how it was said, nothing has been changed, I tried my hardest not to 'butt-in' so that I didn't influence any answer.
Enjoy.

Me "What do you love most about home education?"
Indie: "Well, I don't have to wait to ask a question and I can choose subjects that I want to learn, which I couldn't have done at school. Also, I like that it's just us, so you have a lot at time for us now, rather than the teacher picking other kids, or helping other

kids. It's more fun than school, there's no hassle too, no getting up early and uniforms and stuff. Just way better than school."

Poppy: "Not doing work! Only joking. I love having the choice to do different topics. My science course is so interesting and actually quite fun. I would have thought it was boring before. I can do it in my own time now and I don't have to rush my work, like I felt I needed to at school. Mainly, I love being able to train my dogs. I can do them lots more than I would be able to if I was at high school. Also, I can do a lot of Art now too. I really enjoy Art. My digital drawings have got so much better, now I have time to concentrate on them."

Me "What do you dislike most about home education?"

Indie "One thing. Not having friends about all the time. All day long. The only time I see my friends is when we go to groups, or they come over, or I stay at theirs, or something."

Poppy "Yeah, same as Indie. Covid is mostly to blame for that though, I guess. Covid is annoying. Oh, and I hated it when I told my friends that I was gonna be home educated. They went all weird and avoided me. So, I guess I dislike what people think of home edders too."

Me "What do you want to be when your older?"
Poppy "Architect"

Indie "Jockey! Poppy keeps changing her mind, but I don't."

Poppy "I loved baking, didn't I? I wanted to be a baker and open a bakery, but not now."

Indie "Maybe you can Architect your bakery."

Poppy "Design, Indie!"

Me "What is your favourite club, when Covid isn't about?"

Poppy "Scouts and agility"

Indie "Cubs and Pony Club. I'm not sure which one I enjoy the most. So, I'll say both!"

Me "Ok, in all honesty, what is it like being with your mum 24/7?"

Indie "I like that you are here if I need help. I can talk to you whenever I want and you're fun. I like spending time with you."

Me "Aww Ninny!"

Poppy "It is quite fun. We have a lot of laughs. It can be annoying though. You're like always around! Can I just say something else that I forgot to say? I do like the fact on social media you can block people if they're nasty. At school you can't go around blocking people, you just have to try ignoring them and it's not easy. I love meeting new friends on the internet, especially other home ed kids."

Me "Good point Pop."

Me "What is your favourite project so far?"

Poppy "Definitely not the Titanic! That was pointless. Indie chose that topic because she had already done it at school and it was easy for her. She knew everything before we learnt it. The Bee project was my favourite."

Indie (laughing) "Yep, I so did! Planets! The best project ever, you even let us stick those foam planets to the wall.."

Poppy "Yeah for like two weeks until she regretted it!"

Indie "Oh, I liked them it was so much fun! That reminds me I want to paint my desk, it's ugly!"

Me "So girls, school or home ed?"
Poppy "Errr.... Home ed."
Indie "HOME ED!"
Piper "School."
Poppy "Piper you haven't even been to school."
Piper "HOME ED!"

Home ed and four legs
@homeedandfourlegs

💬 Snippets of my blog page

I have picked some of my favourite Facebook posts for this book.
Amongst all of the random posts on my Facebook page, there are some useful ones.
Some of it may just be repetitive, but some may be really informative.
Others may just make you laugh!

A LONG POST 🙈
But one that I've needed to write for a while. It'll be pinned to the top from now on.

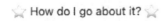 ⭐ How do I go about it? ⭐

The age old question. The one that swims around in my inbox on a daily basis.
How do I start Home Education?

Well firstly, the most important thing is you're thinking about it. That's part of the journey already done because if you are considering home Ed you're probably the right person for the job.
Your reason behind home Ed is your own. It is not something that needs justification, it's not a corner to be fought or a battle to be won. If you want or feel the need to home Ed then it's your choice. Remember, it is a parents responsibility to get/give their children an education. School is an opt in choice, so you can opt out.

Am I clever enough to do it? Will I manage?
Well, did you go to school? Did you gain a GCSE, or at least sit them? You're only required to get your kids to GCSE level, ideally. You are not required to teach them surgery or how to fly a rocket to the moon. If you went to school, all you are doing is telling them what you already know. The thing is home education opens up little minds and you find yourself learning way more things than they'd ever learn at school, so you end up learning too. After all, if you don't know something learn with them, find it out together.
There are plenty of different kinds of families that home Ed. Some home Ed all their kids, some home Ed one whilst the others are in school, some work full or part time around home Ed (superhuman!!), some get tutors or full online

learning and some like me have decided to take on the whole shabangle themselves!

There's also lots of different ways to home educate. I don't like the term homeschool so I use it loosely. I don't think you can replicate school at home and I'm in no way a teacher, but some people do actually try and replicate the structure of school and they are probably the more routine based, structured home edders. Then you have people like me who have some structure but it's very relaxed. We do as we please, run with ideas and as long as the kids are learning I'm happy. We do work and have a semi strict routine but we can also drop a day and do farm things. We don't do normal school hours, we only do about 3 hours of formal work on any one day. Then on top of that we do lots of projects and topic work and try and find ways of learning that doesn't involve a pen and paper. Then there are the radicals.. the "unschoolers". They have very little, if any structure. The kids learn things when they want too. They don't force any type of learning on their child and the child is free to learn life skills without the need of a "lesson". The unschoolers are a vast range of people, you get the simple hippy unschoolers and then you get the proper radical unschoolers.

None of these home educating ways are better than the other, it's just purely what suits you. I advise you get some books, join Home Education U.K. Facebook page and seriously have a think about your route and what will suit your kid and you.

So you've chosen to home school. What to do first? Well firstly you've got to make your school aware. You don't have to give much notice but you do have to make them aware of your choice to home educate and that you want them to take your child(ren) off the school register in accordance with the Education (Pupil Registration) Regulation 2016

with the Education (Pupil Registration) Regulation 2016 section 8(1)(d) for mainstream schools. (There are templates for these letters online, pm me for the link).You should state the date you wish this to happen and that's it. It is the schools responsibility to inform the Local authority (LA). If your child is not of school age and isn't registered into a nursery or preschool then you don't have to do anything. When a letter for you school choices comes, just don't send it back, or send it back with a letter in reply to say you have decided to home educate.
And that's it. Rather simple.
After a short period the LA will get in touch with you, ask you to fill in some forms and have a meeting. Most if not all home Ed parents, file the letter carefully in the bin and don't ever speak to the LA, but I wrote them a lovely letter explaining my reasons for home educating, what I was intending to do (briefly) and that I wasn't in need of a visit just yet. They were very happy.

Now you've got your kid at home and your looking at each other twiddling your thumbs thinking Oh Sh*t!!.. what do you do now? Well seriously this won't be happening. In all honesty I would encourage you to go have some fun. Take some time off and let your kids be kids. They will learn whilst having fun and if they get interested in something, regardless how little, run with it. You'll soon find yourself falling into homeschooling. Once the initial period is over you can initiate your plan of action, however you have decided to home school. It doesn't hurt if you adapt it or change it, actually I feel this is a brilliant thing.
There are no exams to sit. There are no numbers to meet or boxes to tick. With home Ed the world is seriously your oyster. You can holiday when you want, learn when you want, and basically as long as your children are receiving some kind of education in accordance with their age, then you're doing a good job.

Home Ed kids don't sit SATs. They are able to sit GCSEs but it's more likely they'll sit iGCSEs, which is the same thing only a bigger exam because they don't do the GCSE course work. The "I" stands for international. These can actually be sat at any age and at any exam centre/school/college that will allow it.
 There are such things as 14-16 college courses and there's always online courses as well, plus apprenticeships.

I hope you've found this useful. Feel free to ask anything you're not sure about and please get yourself onto Home Education U.K. Facebook page – a great resource with a lot of knowledgeable Home Ed parents.

Good luck
Hannah xx

🖒 Like   💬 Comment   ➢ Share

Home ed and four legs
29 Feb 2020 · Instagram · 🌐

My baby Bellatrix Le strange. Isn't she gorgeous #mygirl
#eldest #theonethatmademeamama #gorgeousgirl
#harrypotterparty #friends #partytime

 38   6 comments

Home ed and four legs
27 Oct 2020 · Instagram · 🌐

When searching for the Whyman-Naveh children, one must first follow the wet and muddy dog, to the wet and muddy place, where the wet and muddy children are!
#playingintherain #wetandmuddy #growingup #playoutside #thisishomeed
#homeeducationlookslikethis #wellingtonboot
#thebiglabradoodle

Home ed and four legs
15 Apr 2020 · Instagram · 🌐

Today was full of lambs and lamb cuddles. We were all helping Poppy tag and move her lambs out onto the meadow. Indie was doing the writing/recording, Poppy and I were doing the chasing and the tagging and Piper was doing the vital cuddling.. A-TEAM!
#homeeducationlookslikethis #ATeam #girlscandoanything #shepherdesses #weareawesome #shadowthorpe #shadowthorpesheep #herdwicksheep #southdownsheep #greyfacedartmoors #cuddles #homeeducation

Home ed and four legs
19 Mar 2020 · Instagram · 🌐

The girls have been outdoors all morning, helping with jobs outside, mucking out and playing on their bikes. Now it's time for some project work.

At the moment it's hard to decide on a topic so we agreed to go back across all the topics we did this past year and make lapbooks. Lapbooks are a great way to store your work, document and also remember what you're learning, purely because it's very crafty. I will do a video of some finished lapbooks later.

Twinkl have an amazing offer on at the moment due to the virus.. if you're interested in lapbooks there are loads of printables and templates on there!!

#lapbooks #homeed #homeeducation #twinkl #projects #projectworks #homeeducator #mygirls #homeedmama

Home ed and four legs
23 Mar 2020 ·

Someone asked for a schedule for her 3yo.
So I gave her mine... 😵🦇😂

    4 h   Like   Reply

   Write a reply...

    Hannah Whyman-Naveh
    My schedule for my almost 3yo is

    8:30 breakfast
    9am -6pm play/lunch/snacks
    7pm Bed

    That's a typical day 🤣🤣

    4 h   Like   Reply   17

   Write a reply...

 28   2 comments

  👍 Like   💬 Comment   ↪ Share

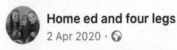

Home ed and four legs

2 Apr 2020 · 🌐

It has been a year to the day since we deregistered our girls from school. It has been an utterly amazing year and I really wish I had done it so much sooner. I used to be so worried about the ifs and buts, whether I was clever enough or if the girls would even listen to me. Now all those worries have vanished, we have our own little home Ed world and it works perfectly for us. We are forever learning 🩶

The point of this blog was to show the good, the bad and the ugly of Home education and although I think I have done that, I still feel there is so much more to be said. The amount of messages I receive from mums who want to know more about home education is crazy, it's always the same questions and worries.

At this precise moment the country finds themselves in this false home schooling routine. It's quite sad that most people will think this isolation schooling is the real thing, it couldn't be further from the truth. We have downed tools for a little while and I must say it's been an eye opener just to see how much my girls have changed this past year. Poppy will happily cook a meal, indie will happily take on a task alone and Piper is blossoming. Here's to many more years of home edding.

Thank you to my hubby who listened to my moaning and went along with this crazy lifestyle, even though he thought I was going crazy! Thanks to Mum and Dad who basically egged me on entirely!

Thank you to those of you who have helped us with this journey. From the fabulous mums from school who stayed friends with us (Gemma mainly), those of you who still invite the girls to parties and sleepovers, those of you who have

Thank you to my hubby who listened to my moaning and went along with this crazy lifestyle, even though he thought I was going crazy! Thanks to Mum and Dad who basically egged me on entirely!

Thank you to those of you who have helped us with this journey. From the fabulous mums from school who stayed friends with us (Gemma mainly), those of you who still invite the girls to parties and sleepovers, those of you who have been a massive support for me and those of you who haven't - you've all spurred me on to do this, and not give up!

My girls are wonderfully wild and free thanks to Home Ed 🏠 a journey in itself that I'm happy to have leaped into 🤱

👍❤️ 69   3 comments 3 shares 🌐 ▾

Home ed and four legs
14 Apr 2020 · 🌐

Isolation schooling vs home education

Yikes. I hope you are all surviving Mamas. Even if your babies are behaving, I hope you're coping with your other halves!! 🔪 👨

Now, I have had a few messages regarding home educating your kids after the lockdown (which will most likely mean September, a new school year!)
Well firstly, that's great!! You're thinking about home educating. I think you're mad because this current situation is draining, it's nothing like real home ed and I think it would even put me off! 😂 BUT, wow, if you are really considering it then good on you!

Whilst I'm very pleased there are some Mamas who love this extra time with their kids and are somehow embracing the forced lockdown, I still worry that some people still aren't quite realising the difference between isolation schooling and home education. Last thing I want to do is put anyone off, but I also don't want you set up for failure.
Besides the fact Home edders are always out and about, socialising (oooer!!), going to groups etc, which is not reflected right now, there's other important things to think about...

Firstly, home education is not supported by a school, governing body or such like, which isolation schooling is. Your school kids have their work packs, school updates, work set by teachers and a port of call if a parent gets stuck. Home edders do not have this. We are on our own. It's a hard thing for many people to get their head around and this is often what puts people off home educating in the first place. There is no school or authority setting work and the brunt of that is on the parent.

Then there's the financial side. At the moment a lot of the subscription companies like Twinkl, toucan boxes and such like, are free or reduced in price. This is not the case for home edders. When we go back to normal, all the prices of these things will also go back to normal. We won't have Joes PE session each morning, we won't have free tuition online and we won't have all the hand outs that you isolation schoolers are currently getting. We pay for everything and financially, it can get pricey, hence why normally home edders try to do as much as they can without the help of subscriptions and online tutoring. Saying that, school can also get pricey but in different ways.

Then of course, the most important thing to remember is, home educators are NOT teachers. We facilitate kids learning but we do not teach. It's an entirely different concept of learning and it's and entirely different way of living. Isolation schooling is mimicking school at home (home work) but home education starts when the child wakes in the morning and stops when they go to sleep. Even in the most structured home Ed home they are learning life skills all day long, every waking moment and through several different normal everyday tasks. For many there is no set timetable and in quite a few HE homes, there's no curriculum to follow. Our children have chores and they don't do "work", they learn because they want too. It takes time, a long time to get them into this frame of mind, much longer than the last 3 weeks of lockdown.

Now, if you are seriously considering home education and you feel you can cope with all the above (you can), then please please please stop schooling. Stop. Keep your kids safe, do short bursts of home work and around that just read books, make cakes, watch movies, talk, build Lego houses. Honestly, you will experience home education much more if you just stop.

Don't try too hard Mamas, and keep your babies safe

#holidaypicture
#bettertimes
#homeeducation
#isoltaionschoolingisnothomeschooling
#homeedlookslikethis

Home ed and four legs
16 Apr 2020 · 🌐

•••

Exploring the meadow this morning - jumping in the spring and counting goose eggs 🥚 lots of fun to be had on the meadow 🌾

Home ed and four legs
6 May 2020 · Instagram · 🌐

My whole world in one photo 🙈
This time sure does make you realise what you've got. It's very easy to take things for granted normally, but not at the moment. Lockdown life is at a much slower pace.

Currently feeling very grateful 😊
#family #isolation #myworld #lockdownlife #stillworking
#stillworktodo✔️

Home ed and four legs
7 May 2020 · Instagram · 🌐

Life's always pretty awesome with a cardboard box and a set of keys 🗝️

#imagination #cardboardbox #cardboardboxfun #toddlerlife

Home ed and four legs

16 Jun 2020 · 🌐

I'm sure plenty of on lookers watch my kids and think they play all day. Well yep they do, but they're also learning. We do a variety of things, which all surrounds learning, whether it's feeding the horses or sheep, pricing up and stamping eggs, making a cake, building something to use on the farm. They're learning and having to use their brain. Obviously they have to work things out for themselves, it would be easier for me to just do the tasks for them but then they wouldn't learn at all.

For example, if I say to Indie can you put a third of that bale in Paddy's stable, that's learning. She has to work out how much a third is (fractions) and she has to carry it to the stable (physical). Another example, making all corners of a hen house right angles (maths and woodwork). Indie has taken a huge interest in all things hands on, whether it's fixing a bike (engineering) or hammering a nail (construction).

As well as all this they also get their core subjects chucked in by doing subjects on their own interests.. Poppy is doing her IGCSE in double science. The writing helps with her English, and obviously maths and science are mixed in there. Whilst Indie is doing her equine courses. The course work helps with her English and as it's all online she also gains endless computing skills.

Basically, there is the ability to learn in everything we do, all day long. Actually they're probably gaining more knowledge than sitting, staring at a text book. However, that doesn't mean there isn't a great amount of work on my behalf. As I said above, either Idan or I have to be there to answer questions, push them to learn and also back off from doing it all for them.

Here's indie helping her dad put a new shed up. Can't get a much better wood work or construction lesson if you tried
This is our home ed.

#homeedlookslikethis #homeeducation #ukhomeed #kidsthatdo #builds #learningallthetime #skills

Feel free to share.. might actually help someone

Home ed and four legs
2 May 2020 · 🌐

Indies hens lay an array of colours! 🐔

Home ed and four legs
8 Jul 2020 · Instagram · 🌐

Piper made a bee and a bee hive 🐝 with her toucan box today! #toucan #toucanboxes #learningthroughplay #homeedkids #homeeducation

133

Home ed and four legs
8 Jul 2020 · 🌐

"Lockdown ain't much different for you..."

How many times have I heard this one?
Nah, I usually act like there's a pandemic, stop my kids from leaving the farm to play with friends and become a recluse 🙄.

Of course it is different. It's different for everyone. Obviously now, there is light at the end of the tunnel but for a few months we have all been suffering with cabin fever, both home edders and not home edders. I am very grateful for the space I have here and it has made me more aware of what we actually have. The idea of spending 12 weeks with 3 kids in a small house with limited garden, or a flat, would drive me insane and I must say those parents who have managed are hero's.

Lockdown has brought good and bad for all of us. Not just the fact that we could not get out but also the worry of what's happening around us, people dying and people being alone. It has been such a scary time. However, it has also made us closer as a family. Idan has had forced time off meaning that Daddy has been home for Indie's birthday, Mother's Day and Father's Day. I can't remember the last time he was home for Father's Day. It's also been a brilliant time for me to concentrate on a few things, like my book. I've started a new business, cut down my dog grooming immensely, which I wanted to do and I've managed to keep up with some home Ed also. We have kept "work" limited purely because it's a weird time for the girls also, bombarding them with a normal amount of work just wasn't fair. Instead we have talked loads and discussed so much, they're probably better people because of the time off.

So as the country starts to go back to normal, I do hope we retain some of the lockdown lessons we've gained. To always respect the NHS, those workers are invaluable. Again, to respect our key workers, who keep us alive and keeps the world turning. To always put time with your family at the top of your list, family is important, and to be thankful for what we have, and what we could loose, rather than what we haven't got 💚 🌈

Home ed and four legs

2 Aug 2020 · Instagram · 🌐

#homeeslookslikethis

Toucan boxes for one child and knitting for another. The best thing about it, they both decided to do it on their own.

#proudmama #learningthroughplay #homeeducation #homeeducationuk #toucanbox #childrenlearn #freetolearn #alwayslearning

Home ed and four legs
11 Sep 2020 · Instagram · 🌐

"Am I good enough to teach my kids?"
Well, I am not a teacher, I'm a facilitator.
I facilitate learning, I make sure there are lots of subjects on offer and I give them the opportunity to learn about them.
So I don't need a degree in teaching because I'm not teaching. The girls have recently started an English lesson with a tutor via Zoom, but otherwise they do no curriculum based subjects, as such.
It's hard to explain, but for example Indie is really into horses so she is on every course related to horses that I can possibly find. Whether it is pony club, which covers the practical side, "PE" in school terms, or an online course which covers her maths and English. Honestly, there is learning in everything they do and I can't stop banging on about it.
So to answer your question, maybe not, but you're not teaching. Home edders just need the space, the time and the resources to learn and then they'll learn for themselves.

Photos professionally take by Piper yesterday, so I won't take the credit!! 😂😂

#noteachershere #teachersrockthough #totalsaints
#couldntdoit #facilitator #homeedmama #homeedlife

137

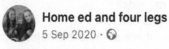

Home ed and four legs
5 Sep 2020 · 🌐

My kids, I'm sorry

To my eldest. I'm sorry.
I'm sorry for expecting you to grow up fast. For pushing you to reach every milestone and to push you harder to reach goals than needed. I'm sorry for expecting too much of you. You get more of my frustration than your other siblings. I'm sorry that you're going through all this first. My first baby, my first true love, my first toddler, my first pre-teen and so on. You are more than a "first" but I was also a "first", a first time mum and at times I was scared. Scared to do things wrong. Scared to let you down. Scared of not being a brilliant mum. I'm sorry for over reacting when you fell over, or cried, or felt unwell. I was new to all this. You are utterly wonderful, you made me a mum.

To my middle child. I'm sorry.
Sorry you're in the middle. Not the eldest and not the baby. I'm sorry for hand me downs, they're perfectly fine you see and yet you deserve your own "firsts". I'm sorry for not being elated at your firsts. I'd been through it all before and having an older one as well meant life was already in the fast lane. I'm sorry for not letting you be the baby forever. You are more than enough and I love you with all my heart. You're not feral, you're just free and wild and amazing.

To my youngest. I'm sorry.
Sorry that I "baby" you. You're my last so I want to savour the moments. Im sorry that I don't want you to hit milestones, it means you're growing up, too fast. I'm sorry that you want to be older, and catch up with the others, but can't. I'm sorry for always being occupied. You've never had me to yourself and yet you have me more than you realise. I'm sorry for being relaxed when you bump your head or graze a knee, I know these will mend quick and a cuddle is all that's needed. I'm sorry for not buying the latest fad baby item or toy, my others didn't need them.

I'm not sorry for loving all of you, with all my heart, as individuals and as one. You are mine, you are a piece of me and you are my everything 🖤

Home ed and four legs
21 Nov 2019 · 🌐

When you're out for lunch with 3 hoolies (indie didn't fit in) and you get comments on how well behaved they are and how unhooligan like 🙈😇

Worth more to me than any SATs test..

Home ed and four legs
28 Oct 2020 · Instagram · 🌐

Monday's exercise.. digging up fodderbeet for the sheep!

🥴 👌 #digdigdig #comeonegirls #fillthattrailer #fodderbeet #teamworkmakesthedreamwork💯

Home ed and four legs

26 Nov 2020 · 🌐

Finally realised where Indie gets her hands on approach to life from.

I got sent this photo recently from a member of Idans kibbutz.

This is a very young Idan in Israel. Apparently he was sent to help pull a tractor out but ended up making the situation worse 😂 before it got better.

I'm afraid to say, he still has this way of working (sorry Idan 🙃) he is always tinkering with things and finding jobs to do and he doesn't give up if it fails the first time. He is honestly the hardest worker I know and he never sits still.

The ultimate home Ed daddy, he installs a lot of skills into our girls and teaches them to be hands on. Not many 11 and 9yos can back a quad and trailer.

He is not one to boast about his knowledge and he doesn't purport to know-it-all, even though he's a very knowledgable man. I get mad at him for having bits of machinery everywhere but if I'm in a pickle with the quad or my horse lorry, he's rather handy. Indie is the same. No she isn't a fan of writing or doing anything remotely paper based but she's learning through her hands, from the best 🖤

Home ed and four legs
8 Sep 2020 · Instagram · 🌐

Indie Rose.. the one who makes me grey #indierosie #feral
#superspesh #homeedkid #homeedkidsrock

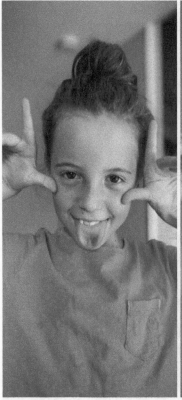 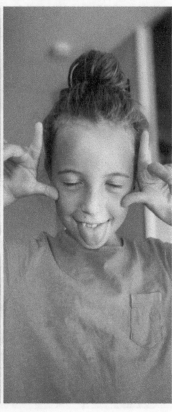

Home ed and four legs
28 Dec 2020 · Instagram · 🌐

It's that time of year when I sit and contemplate what the girls should actually be learning over the next year. Eventhough I'm only semi structured and prefer a relaxed feel to home Ed, I always manage to slip lessons, tasks and projects in somewhere. It's harder with repeated lockdowns because days out get cancelled and plans changed but I roll with it. This year Piper will be starting to have a more structured roll and will have some little tasks, which I'm finding she's asking for now anyway.

It's a great chance to get an idea on actually how the girls have developed over the year, not just with their education but life skills also. Like for example leaving them alone to do things themselves, to get jobs done without me constantly over them. Poppy definitely finds that rewarding as it gives her more responsibility and make her feel more grown up. Indie still needs a bit of a kick up the arse when it comes to anything that isn't shaped like a horse.. if that girl was any more laid back she would fall over 🙈

Oh and it's also time for a clear out, hence the bin bags (don't worry it's clothes going in the charity bins ♻️)

#homeedmama #homeedlife #laidbacklife #homeeducator #homeedkids #educatingathome

145

Home ed and four legs
29 Dec 2020 · 🌐

Reasons why I home educate.

1) it's a bully free zone 🔘. I have no risk of my kids getting bullied at school, meaning low self esteem and poor education through lack of concentration. Bullying can still happen online but my girls learn that "online" can easily be "offline" by being blocked, turned off or ignored. Hard to do that when your bully is in your classroom over a thousand hours a year.

2) no school run 🏃. I don't think this needs any explaination and in my opinion it should be at the top of the list!

3) I get to give my kids a more rounded education. They still do maths and English but they also learn about real things, like how to survive life rather than, how to pass this test.

4) So they spend more time with their Dad. Having a dad who works every single weekend and sometimes during the week, meant they only saw him in passing. These days they spend a lot of time with him and he has a massive impact on their home life and education.

5) They are more social.. don't laugh! Yeah I know you're probably thinking, but home Ed kids are socially awkward. Nah. They're not, well not the ones I've met anyhow. My girls speak to anyone now, they make friends easier than they ever used too. Before they had their group of friends and that was it. Now they have friends the other side of the country that they FaceTime each night, they have old friends from school that they see in holidays, they have friends from their groups, they have made friends in adults, they talk to everyone regardless of the situation, could be the lady in the shop or a new tutor.

Home education gives kids something to talk about.

6) they have more time to concentrate on what they are passionate about. Poppy's passion changes like the wind and that's ok, at the moment she wants to be an architect when she's older so we are helping her educate herself in what she needs to become an architect. If she decides it isn't for her she hasn't lost anything, only gained. Indie wants to be a jockey 🐎 or at least work with horses, so she is doing loads of equine online courses and riding at every opportunity. Piper, god knows what she wants to be (probably a sky diving instructor 🪂) but she will work it out as she gets older and I will tailor her education towards that.

7) I spend time with my girls. Christ this is a hard one. I spend time pulling my hair out, I shout, I am constantly tidying up and I get so angry at how much they argue at times. BUT, it's family life and I get to spend it with them, knowing them entirely. With that, I also give them a lot of time without me, to be responsible, take on tasks and get a sense of achievement when it's finished. I rarely say "be careful" these days, they are careful and they shouldn't be fearful of trying new things or doing things alone.

There's no expectations. We are us and we live each day as it comes.

8) my free spirits get to be free.
Uninterrupted freedom. To learn, to explore, to be silly, to gain confidence, to not worry about peer pressures, to decide who they are and to do all this is in a beautiful farm yard full of space and trees and animals. Jumping in mud, climbing, exploring, riding, running.

What more could a kid want

 94   25 comments 11 shares

Home ed and four legs

7 Jan · Instagram · 🌐

• • •

Piper is colouring in some of my colouring pages. These are all available on the website for FREE, so feel free to download them for your little ones.

HannahwhymannavehAuthor.com

#freebies #itallhelps #smallthings #colouringpages #freecolouringpages #homeeducationuk #homeedmama #kidscraftstagram

This book would not have been possible without the following people:

My wonderful **mum** for being my proofreader several times and for encouraging me.

Liz - For being the best editor I could have found.

Special Little Feet by Karla Davis
What an amazing photographer you are. Thank you for allowing me to use your photos.

Fakenham Prepress Solutions
For taking my design and turning it into a professional looking cover. Brilliant to work with you.

Idan
Thank you for taking on this amazing life with me and listening to me ramble on about writing, even more than I talk about ponies!

My three beautiful girls
I hope you are proud of me.
I am so proud of you all.
Home ed kids rock and I love you all 3000!

Hannah Whyman-Naveh is the author and illustrator of the childrens' book series ***Piper and Minnie.***
These short stories are loosely based on Hannah's youngest daughter Piper and her pet chicken, Minnie. Hannah is currently writing more books for the series and hopes to publish them during 2021.

The following books can be purchased from all major book stores:

Piper and Minnie - Minnie goes missing

Piper and Minnie - Minnie's vet adventure

Piper and Minnie - Minnie finds a reindeer

HannahwhymannavehAuthor.com
Shadowthorpe illustrations

Lightning Source UK Ltd.
Milton Keynes UK
UKHW040739030321
379707UK00001B/35